TEMPER TAMING TIPS

The College Student's Guide to Anger Intelligence™

Neca C. Smith

Life Intelligence Publications
Atlanta, Georgia

TEMPER TAMING TIPS
The College Student's Guide to Anger Intelligence™

Copyright © 2011 by Neca C. Smith

Published by Life Intelligence Publications, Atlanta, GA
USA

ISBN 978-0615512853

Acknowledgments

Special thanks to Asiah K. Wolfolk-Manning, Tammie Bailey-Fults, Yakema Hicks-Williams and Ivan Whitted II for their encouragement, advice, assistance and efforts in this endeavor.

Acknowledgment

Acknowledgments

Special thanks to Asiah K. Wolfolk-Manning, Tammie Bailey-Fults, Yakema Hicks-Williams and Ivan Whitted II for their encouragement, advice, assistance and efforts in this endeavor.

Acknowledgments

Table of Contents

Introduction

College is a time meant for self-exploration, discovery, and even fun (when time permits). However, it is also a time of rapid change, difficulty, and challenge for a student. Oftentimes, while undergoing the struggles of a college life, we may not know the best way to handle these challenges. There are also times when we may even be blind to our own issues with anger. Anger is a natural emotion that everyone experiences, but knowing how to control it is essential to both social interaction and maintaining a comfortable lifestyle. If you plan to do anything in life besides lying in bed with the covers over your head then you are going to need to know how to respond when life and people make you upset. My hope is that this little book will get you started on the right path towards a successful and stress-free future with the help of these 26 tips to tame your uncontrollable temper. Here's to your college success!!!

TEMPER TAMING TIPS

1

Don't Let Your Attitude Damage Your Potential

TEMPER TAMING TIPS
The College Student's Guide to
Anger Intelligence™

Don't Let Your Attitude Damage
Your Potential

Marcus Vick is the younger brother of Philadelphia Eagles quarterback, Michael Vick. Though Michael has had his share of legal problems, his brother Marcus exhibited some real temper control problems while in college. While in high school, Marcus was one of the top quarterback prospects in the country and was heavily recruited by major universities with top notch football programs. He decided on Virginia Tech, his brother Michael's alma mater, and received a full scholarship. He made an awesome showing at the beginning of his college career but that all ended when he had on and off the field temper problems.

While playing in the Gator Bowl in 2006, he displayed unsportsmanlike conduct when he intentionally stomped the leg of a player from the opposing team. He was permanently dismissed from the team. Marcus responded to being released by saying that the dismissal didn't matter since he was going to the NFL. Three days after this incident he was charged with three counts of brandishing a firearm at a group of teenagers. Marcus did go to the NFL. He played for the Miami Dolphins - one season.

Marcus Vick's temper and attitude kept him from achieving greatness in college and professional football. He had all the potential and athletic prowess an athlete could ask for but it did not matter because he allowed his temper and attitude to ruin his chances.

What will having a bad temper keep YOU from achieving?

2

Give 100% the First Time!

TEMPER TAMING TIPS
The College Student's Guide to
Anger Intelligence™

Give 100% the First Time!

You've just finished your first research paper for your Intro to Sociology class. You waited until the last minute to do the research and were careless and hasty in your writing. You're excited and exhausted at the same time. You are excited because it's done but exhausted by the last minute energy you put into it. You're back in class and you get your grade. But the professor didn't even give you a grade…in fact he gave you an incomplete! In order to get a grade you have to make the corrections he suggested. How do you respond? You may get upset and angry and finish the paper. You might meet with the professor to protest the recommendations. You may do him a favor and not make the changes at all. How can you make sure that this never happens again?

Give it your best the first time! **Procrastination, laziness, and unpreparedness are the kinds of qualities that cause unnecessary anger.** In the scenario, had you been prepared and thorough, there would not have been a reason to be upset with anyone…yourself or the professor!

TEMPER TAMING TIPS

Where in your life do you realize that you haven't given your best? Write them down and then list ways you can do better the next time.

Less than 100%	100% or more!

3

Accept Others for Who They Are

TEMPER TAMING TIPS
The College Student's Guide to
Anger Intelligence™

Accept Others for Who They Are

"**M**y roommate should have asked my permission to use my laptop!"

"I have to finish this paper by tomorrow or I'm screwed!"

"I must become a member of this sorority or nobody will like me."

"My mom ought to just leave me alone about my grades… it's not that big of a deal."

Ever thought or said any of these statements or anything similar? Go back and look for the words **have to, ought to, must, and should** in the statements above. These are **demandingness statements**. Demandingness is the idea that everything should and must your way. These kinds of thoughts are unreasonable expectations that we hold of ourselves, others and the world.   In other words, we expect the world to revolve around all of our needs and wants and when it doesn't we often become so angry it harms our relationships.   I remember when I was in college; I had very unreasonable expectations of my boyfriend back then. I thought he should do things the way I did them, like all the movies I liked, be interested in all the things I was interested in and when he didn't I would get extremely upset and annoyed. Because of that attitude, our relationship lacked genuine respect and communication. The reality of it was that he didn't HAVE to think, do, or be the way I wanted him to. Just as our partners, parents, friends, or classmates don't have to think, do or be what we want them to.

It is important to learn how to accept others and situations for who or what they are (right now) and NOT for who you want them to be.

Demandingness		
The idea that everything should and must go a certain way. Unreasonable expectations that we hold of ourselves, others, and the world in general.		
Key Words: Should, must, need to, ought, have to, etc.		
Demanding Thought→	Response→	Realistic Thought
1."I shouldn't have to deal with these headaches!"	Identify what are needs and what are wants.	1. "This job comes with its share of problems at times."
2."Traffic shouldn't be so heavy at this hour."	Realize your preferences.	2. "It's 4pm, so I expect a good amount of traffic."
3." It should not be that hard!"	Learn to accept others and situations as they are, NOT as you would like them to be.	3. "This is not easy."
What are your own demanding thoughts? Add them here!		

4

Judge the Behavior, Not the Person

Judge the Behavior, Not the Person

People sometimes behave in ways that are strange to us or in ways we just plain don't like. When they do this we might respond by **condemning** them – that is, the thought of putting others or yourself down. When people don't meet your expectations you feel as though they deserve to be punished, put down or talked about. The reality is this - MOST people you encounter when you get to college will be a LOT different from anything you've ever experienced and it's OK. You may undergo a bit of a culture shock depending on what background you came from. I know of a student who attended elementary, middle, and high schools that were predominately African-American. He chose to attend a college that was much more multi-cultural. He admitted to being initially stunned by the diversity of backgrounds of the other students. However, he made the choice to have an open mind and attitude of tolerance to connect and make friends with those he initially deemed as different. Be careful not to judge others too harshly because they are different from you. These kinds of judgments are where racism, sexism, and all other kinds of "isms" are born.

Learning to rate the actions of someone instead of judging them is the best way to handling condemning thoughts. When you change your thoughts to focus on the behavior and not the person, you will find yourself less frustrated with the actions of others. Also, be careful in condemning others because you might find yourself guilty of the same behavior at some point. What kind of treatment would you like in regards to YOUR unbecoming behaviors?

Condemning

The thought of putting yourself or others down. Beliefs that stem from the idea that people who don't meet my expectations or some moral obligation deserve to be punished.

Condemning Thought→	Response→	Realistic Thought
1. "He flew off the handle again, he's hopeless." 2. "Every time I try, I fail." 3. "My coworker is stupid!" **What are your own condemning thoughts? Add them here!**	**Rate the behavior not the person.** **Learn to accept others and yourself.**	1. "He seems to get upset a lot." 2. "Sometimes I fail, but I'll keep trying." 3. "Sometimes my co-worker bothers me by what she says."

5

Think about Your Thinking

TEMPER TAMING TIPS
The College Student's Guide to
Anger Intelligence™

Think About Your Thinking!

D id you know that it is your thinking that causes your temper to flare? Yeah, that's right! It's not your boyfriend's text message or your roommates comment about your outfit - it's your thoughts. Greek philosopher Epictetus says that "Men are disturbed not by things but of the views which they take of them."

Your anger is not about the person you're upset with - it's about what you are thinking regarding the person. If you think happy thoughts you usually feel happy, right? If you think angry thoughts you will probably feel angry. So mind your thoughts - that is think about your thinking.

Here is a wonderful story that illustrates this point –

"Jerry was always in a good mood and always had something positive to say. When someone would ask him how he was doing, he would reply, 'If I were any better, I would be twins!' When asked why he was so positive, Jerry replied, 'Each morning I wake up and say to myself, Jerry, you have two choices today. You can choose to be in a good mood or you can choose to be in a bad mood. I choose to be in a good mood. Each time something bad happens, I can choose to be a victim or I can choose to learn from it. I choose to learn from it. Every time someone comes to me complaining, I can choose to accept their complaining or I can point out the positive side of life. I choose the positive side of life.'

While at work Jerry was held up at gun point and shot by three armed robbers. Six months after the accident when asked how he was, he replied, 'If I were any better, I'd be twins! Honestly, as I lay on the floor, I remembered that I had two choices: I could choose to live or I could choose to die. I chose to live.'

Jerry continued, '...the paramedics were great. They kept telling me I was going to be fine. But when they wheeled me into the ER and I saw the expressions on the faces, in their eyes, I read 'he's a dead man.' 'There was a big burly nurse shouting questions at me,' said Jerry. 'She asked if I was allergic to anything. Yes,' I replied. The doctors and nurses stopped working as they waited for my reply. I took a deep breath and yelled, 'Bullets!' Over their laughter, I told them, 'I am choosing to live. Operate on me as if I am alive, not dead.'"

Jerry made a choice to have a positive mindset, even in the midst of adversity.

What are some negative thoughts you have regularly?
What are some positive thoughts that you can choose to
replace them with?

Negative Thought	Positive Alternative Thought

6

Don't Get Mad, Get Motivated!

TEMPER TAMING TIPS
The College Student's Guide to
Anger Intelligence™

Don't Get Mad, Get Motivated!

U se your anger for good! "How can you do that?" you ask. Anger is not designed to destroy, harm or hurt. Anger is an emotion that is designed to motivate you to change something in your environment or situation. For example, when you get annoyed about something - stop thinking about how annoyed you are and who annoyed you. Instead think about how to be less annoyed the next time or how you can change the situation. **Those things that anger us aren't there just to bother us-- they are there to change us - only us and no one else.**

I once heard a story about a king who had a boulder placed on a roadway. The king hid himself and watched to see if anyone would remove the huge rock. Some of the king's wealthiest merchants came by and simply walked around it. Many loudly blamed the king for not keeping the roads clear, but none did anything about getting the big stone out of the way. Then a peasant came along carrying a load of vegetables. On approaching the boulder, the peasant laid down his load and tried to move the stone to the side of the road. After much pushing and straining, he finally succeeded. As the peasant picked up his load of vegetables, he noticed a purse lying in the road where the boulder had been. The purse contained many gold coins and a note from the king indicating that the gold was for the person who removed the boulder from the roadway. The peasant learned what many others never understand. **Every obstacle presents an opportunity to improve one's condition.**

Your anger is like that boulder. It represents an opportunity to improve your condition.

In what ways can you use your anger as a motivator and an opportunity?

What situations or environments anger/annoy you?	What are some ways to improve your situation or environment?

7

Avoid Extreme Thinking

TEMPER TAMING TIPS
The College Student's Guide to
Anger Intelligence™

Avoid Extreme Thinking

Having extremely negative thoughts or making a big deal out of nothing quickly causes us to turn to negative, destructive behavior. Words like "never" or "always" are used to describe things you would consider awful, terrible or horrible. These kinds of thoughts are called awfulizing thoughts. **When you are awfulizing you are making exaggerated statements about an issue that is actually quite believable.**

Have you ever made these statements? "They're always spreading rumors." Or "This is the worst day of my life."Are they really *always* spreading rumors? Do *you* ever partake in the rumor spreading as well? If they are spreading rumors what can you really do about it even if it is about you? Is it really the *worst* day of your life? If it is, then what is one thing you can do to make it better? Do you say this statement often? If so, then what was that *actual worse day*? Have you ever considered the possibility of an even worse day then you experienced?

Learn to think in more realistic terms. There is something called the gray area. **Some things** may honestly be bad but **everything** isn't horrible. Get it?!

Awfulizing

Thinking in extreme negative terms. (Making mountains out of molehills.) They are gross exaggerations about reality.

Key Words: **Terrible, horrible and awful**. Words like **always** and **never** are cues as well.

Awfulizing Thought→	Response→	Realistic Thought
1. *"I can't believe they're gossiping again!"*	Learn to think in realistic, moderate terms	1. *"It's easy to believe they're gossiping again."*
2. *"It's terrible that got a "C" on my paper!* What are your own awfulizing thoughts? Add them here!	Avoid extreme thinking (either positive or negative)	2. *"I didn't get the grade I wanted but I will try harder on the next one."*

8

Tolerate Frustration

TEMPER TAMING TIPS
The College Student's Guide to
Anger Intelligence™

Tolerate Frustration

As I am writing this page I am at a library with an outside patio. After enjoying the breeze and the fresh air and getting some work done a young man comes and sits down at the same table I am sitting at and doesn't acknowledge my "hello". Later he begins to the blast music from his laptop and I ask him to turn it down. Then this individual begins to talk to his computer and bang on his keyboard, obviously upset about what his computer screen is telling him. I admit, I'm pretty annoyed at this point because I wanted to be alone on the library patio. Initially I thought "Oh great, here's this guy about to ruin my entire afternoon." I thought about leaving and going inside. But then I thought "No, I don't want to go in and he's really not bothering me that much." And on top of that this gives me a story about how to increase my ability to tolerate frustration!

When you allow yourself to get frustrated by small incidents or situations that you cannot control, how much more will you become angry about more serious matters? **Accept the reality that there will be minor annoyances in your life every day.** You have a choice to either focus on minor frustrating issues or giving your attention to those issues that are more important. Which will you choose?

Tolerating Frustration

Thought that comes from the expectations that things must go smoothly for us or we will not be able to stand it.

Frustrating Thought→	Response→	Realistic Thought
1. "I cannot stand it when I have to wait in line."	Accept the reality of frustration and keep its "badness" in perspective.	1. "I don't like waiting in line."
2. "I'm going to snap if he asks me another question!" What are your own frustrating thoughts? Add them here!	Expect to experience appropriate negative emotions like annoyance and disappointment. But avoid exaggerating these emotions by telling yourself you can't stand them.	2. "I will be bothered if he continues to ask questions."

9

Be Assertive!

TEMPER TAMING TIPS
The College Student's Guide to
Anger Intelligence™

Be Assertive!

I magine this – You are in the grocery store checkout line and someone comes in and cuts the line in front of you. How do you respond? I know in a situation like this it's hard to keep your mouth closed. Your first thought may be to let them know exactly how you feel but maybe not in the most tactful way – why not? They deserve it, right?

Wrong! In a situation such as this, it makes more sense to respond assertively. **Being assertive when communicating with others is to stand up for your rights without violating the rights of others.** When you are assertive you are intent on understanding others and being understood.

There are a few other styles of communication that you probably use more often than assertive. Check out the styles on the next page – which of these forms of communication do you use most often?

Styles of Communication – Which of these do you use?

Aggressive Communication

A form of communication that focuses on being in control. Aggressive communicators stand up for their rights but do so by violating the rights of others. Words used to describe aggressive communicators are: **arrogant, bully, bossy, domineering, and overbearing.**

Passive Communication

A form of communication that is defined by avoiding conflict and pleasing others. Passive communicators tend to hold in their true feelings and don't stand up for their own rights. Words used to describe passive communicators are: **timid, scared, submissive, apologetic, and indecisive.**

Passive-Aggressive Communication

A form of communication that is defined by indirectly expressing negative or angry feelings. Passive-Aggressive communicators express themselves by appearing cooperative on the surface but show their true feelings by using criticism, procrastination, or even sabotage to undermine others. Words used to describe passive-aggressive communicators are: **sarcastic, manipulative, resentful, and undermining.**

Assertive Communication

A form of communication that focuses on understanding others and being understood by others. Assertive communicators stand up for their rights without violating the rights of others. Words used to describe assertive communicators are: **rational, understanding, honest, fair and responsible.**

10

It's Me, Not You

TEMPER TAMING TIPS
The College Student's Guide to
Anger Intelligence™

There was a young man who always blamed his girlfriend for every negative feeling he had. He would say things like "YOU make me so mad" or "YOU don't care about me". This continued throughout their two year relationship. Eventually, his girlfriend ended the relationship – not because she didn't care about him anymore but because she was sick and tired of being blamed for how he felt.

Romantic relationships begin as a dream come true and sometimes end as your worst nightmare. Many arguments in relationships come about due to a lack of respectful communication. Respectful communication is the same as assertive communication. Remember you when you are pointing at someone there's one finger pointing at them and four pointing back at you.

A way to avoid blaming others is to use "I" statements. "I" statements are the cornerstone of Assertive Communication. They allow individuals to express their feelings, wants, and needs without blaming others for your thoughts and feelings. They also allow individuals to process and express their primary emotions and become responsible for their feelings and desires.

"I" Statements are formulated in this way:

I feel _____*emotion*_____ because/when _____*reason*_____.

I would like _____*desired outcome.*_____

TEMPER TAMING TIPS

Example: I feel **_neglected_** when you **_don't call when you say you will_**. I would like for **_you do what you say you were going to do._**

Construct your own "I" Statements:

1) What is my PRIMARY emotion (besides anger)?

I feel _____

2) Why do I feel this way? What is the reason I feel this emotion?

When/Because _____

3) What reasonable outcome would I like?

I would like _____

Now try this with two more situations:

I feel _____

When/Because _____

I would like _____

I feel _____

When/Because _____

I would like _____

11

Take a Time Out

TEMPER TAMING TIPS
The College Student's Guide to
Anger Intelligence™

Take a Time Out

Sometimes when you get caught in the heat of the moment of an argument, you may do or say something you regret. You may yell and scream, make sarcastic or nasty remarks, you may even fight, kick, punch or destroy things. If you find yourself doing any of these things then taking a time out will be a good technique for you to know.

A time out is used when an argument or conversation is beginning to get out of control. Your heart may be beating fast, you're breathing is rapid, your hands may begin to sweat or you may feel butterflies in your stomach. You may even start yelling or talking louder than you normally do – you might even want to get physical with the person. If any of these are a occurring - use a time out to defuse the anger and diminish the conflict. It is not the same as just walking out because it involves setting rules and guidelines with those significant in our lives.

Rules for Time Out

1. Make a time out contract. Talk the person and agree to use time-outs as a way to manage conflict.
2. Decide on a signal or phrase you will use to signal the need for a time-out. Example: *I need to take a time-out; I can't express myself right now.*
3. Set a time limit beforehand. Give yourself at least an hour but not over 2 hours.
4. Leave immediately or just stop talking if you cannot leave the other person's presence.
5. Come back at the designated time.
6. No drinking or drugs during the time-out.
7. During that time, take a walk or exercise. Also, think about what it is you want to say. Use an "I" statement if appropriate.

Which rules will you use?

12

Respond to Criticism Calmly

TEMPER TAMING TIPS
The College Student's Guide to
Anger Intelligence™

Respond to Criticism Calmly

D o you ever feel like your parents are still trying to tell you what to do? After all you're in college now, you should be able to make your own decisions, right? I remember when I was in high school; my mom said that I wasn't responsible enough and me to be more independent before I went to college, so she made me set my own doctor's appointments. I was sooooo annoyed with her for saying that I wasn't responsible and making me call the doctor's office. When I became a freshman, however, I had to set all my own appointments regarding financial aid, housing, meal plans…you name it. These were easy tasks because my mom made sure I was already prepared. Initially, I felt as though she was being critical but I eventually realized it was constructive criticism. I'm glad I followed her advice now!

So, what is the difference between constructive criticism and destructive criticism?

Destructive criticism is negative feedback that is used to destroy or tear down. They blame, ridicule, belittle and insult and in no way builds you up.

Constructive criticism however is based on positive feedback. It is used to correct in a way that builds up and is intended to bring about the best in you – even when you don't want to listen. Frequently, as a college student, you may feel like your parents are still trying to "tell you want to do" and sometimes it feels like criticism but of the destructive sort. But when you think about what they're saying – consider their intentions – Do they really have your best interest at heart or are they trying to put you down, belittle or insult you?

Here are a few techniques you can use when confronting criticism of any kind.

<u>Broken Record</u>

The Broken Record is an effective technique when setting boundaries if someone is not respecting what you have to say. This is best used in non-personal situations rather than with those with whom you have any kind of personal relationship. It is helpful in avoiding manipulation and arguments. Repeat your statement calmly and exit if need be.

Helpful "Broken Record" Statements:

"No thank you."

"Not today."

"I'm sorry you feel that way."

"We have a different opinion."

"I understand but I'm not interested."

<u>Focus on the Facts</u>

This technique is used when being criticized by focusing on the important facts but ignoring harsh, critical statements by others. Use words like might, maybe, or sometimes.

Example:

You're irrational!

Fogging Response: "Sometimes my thinking isn't rational."

Negative Assertion

Accepting the truth of a criticism and stating it in positive terms.

Example:

You're irrational!

Negative Assertion: **"You're right, sometimes I don't think as clearly as I could."**

Negative Inquiry

When responding to negative criticism, asking for constructive criticism.

Example:

You're irrational!

Negative Inquiry Response: **"Can you tell me what I said that was irrational?"**

13

Write It Down

TEMPER TAMING TIPS
The College Student's Guide to
Anger Intelligence™

Write It Down!

Sometimes it seems like avoiding anger altogether is the best way to handle it. It's just much easier to withdraw by reading or watching TV or playing video games. **Unfortunately, pretending you are not angry about something when you really are upset about it is certain to lead to resentment or bitterness**.

One of the best ways to handle avoidance when you're not necessarily ready to deal with something that is upsetting you is **to write it down and keep it somewhere you can look at it the next day.** Maybe send yourself a reminder to read it. The key here is to acknowledge that you are upset at the moment and then make plans to revisit it again. Avoiding anger can lead to bitterness and grudges. Don't avoid it – acknowledge it and deal with it!

If you are continuously avoiding anger try this exercise. This will allow for some form of expression, particularly if you are not ready to express it yet.

Who are you upset with?	
What are you upset about?	
Why are you upset about it?	

Who are you upset with?	
What are you upset about?	
Why are you upset about it?	

Revisit this activity in a couple of days and decide if you are ready to discuss it with the other party or someone you trust.

14

Don't Let Your Words Hurt

TEMPER TAMING TIPS
The College Student's Guide to
Anger Intelligence™

Don't Let Your Words Hurt

While I was perusing the internet one day, I ran across a blog post that said "Everybody knows how bad my temper is – I mean to know me is to know my attitude. I know what to say to hurt people's feelings AND I'm good at it! And if you're good at it – why not use it!" Wow…was all I could say!

Are you one of these people? A person who doesn't see anything wrong at all with your temper or bad attitude? You don't think it really hurts anyone else? Here is a story that illustrates this point perfectly:

Very long ago there lived a boy who got angry over every little thing. Seeing the boy struggle with his temper, the father called the boy one day and gave him a bag of nails. "Every time you get angry, drive one nail into the wooden fence," said the father. The boy, prone to anger, drove 37 nails into the fence on the first day. On the second, he nailed much less. And as days passed by he slowed down. Finally he realized that it was easier to control his temper than to continue nailing the fence. Then came a day when he didn't use a single nail.

Happy that he had controlled his anger, he went to his father and said, "Father, I haven't lost my temper the whole day." "Good. Now go and pull out all the nails in the fence," said the father. The boy did as told. Now, the fence was full of holes. Then the father took him to the fence, "Can you see the holes in the fence, my dear son.

That's what happens when you get angry and say or do something harmful to someone. It leaves an ugly scar. No matter how many times you say sorry, the wound remains unhealed."

What is the moral of this story? Think about all of the people you hurt when you don't tame your temper.

Write a list of those people who you believe have been hurt by your words. What can you do to avoid hurting them in the future?

15

Get the Best of Your Anger

TEMPER TAMING TIPS
The College Student's Guide to
Anger Intelligence™

Get the Best of Your Anger

" *G*o *ahead and be angry. You do well to be angry—but don't use your anger as fuel for revenge. And don't stay angry. Don't go to bed angry." Ephesians 4:26 The Message Bible*

This scripture from the Bible is helpful to aid you in taming your temper. **Anger is natural, normal and necessary.** It is natural because our bodies and our brains have automatic responses to anger triggers and play major roles in our actions. It is normal because there are things to be justifiably upset about. Everyone gets angry or upset to some degree – you are not abnormal! Finally, it is necessary because anger is designed to motivate us; it lets us know that there is something wrong in our environment that we must do something about it.

As you can see, it's okay to be angry - the issue is not the anger - it is what you do with it. Are your reactions and responses to those things that bother you destructive or constructive? Most of the time our anger is destructive, it destroys our relationships, our reputation and our peace of mind. But when you have constructive anger such as the Civil Rights movement – you may be able to change something bigger than yourself.

In March of 2011, students at Dickinson College in Carlisle, Pennsylvania were upset and frustrated about the schools handling of sexual assault and date rape cases on campus. After experiencing unsettling sexual assaults on campus, students made demands on the school's administration to make policy changes to deal with these kinds of situations more effectively. Instead of becoming violent or making threats, 200 of the students staged a sit-in inside of the school's administration building. Their actions led to a meeting with the college's president and changes to the school's sexual assault policy.

List some ways you can use YOUR anger for good.

16

Mean What You Say

TEMPER TAMING TIPS
The College Student's Guide to
Anger Intelligence™

Mean What You Say

How important is communication to you? Do you know what part effective communication plays in heated arguments? Learning effective communication will help you excel in your relationships with your professors, family, with friends, and even in your new career. In anger, our communication is disrupted due to misunderstandings.

Communication is successful ONLY when the message you send is the same message that is received. In other words, you are only communicating effectively if people understand what you intend for them to understand. When we are frustrated, it can be hard to express what we are feeling. What you have said is not what you meant. Being able to communicate your thoughts and feelings adequately and to listen to what others think and feel is the sign of a great communicator!

For your exercise, identify the Angry Verbal Communication tactic that you currently use by circling it. Next, circle the Productive Verbal Communication tactics you will begin practicing.

Angry Verbal Communication	Productive Verbal Communication
Yelling, Screaming	Calmly talking out the issue
Interrupting the speaker	Listening to the speaker before you respond
Finishing the speakers sentences	Waiting for the speaker to finish
Not asking questions	Asking questions to clarify and understand the speaker
Asking questions without waiting for a response	Listening for the answers in order to obtain a response
Tuning out	Listening

17

Watch Your Body Talk

TEMPER TAMING TIPS
The College Student's Guide to
Anger Intelligence™

Watch Your Body Talk

When you are angry do you show it rather than say it? According to different sources 90% of our communication is non-verbal. That is – does your facial expression or body language say more than your words do? Body language, facial expressions, tone of voice, and gestures are all of what make up non-verbal communication.

For instance, have you ever greeted someone and asked the how they are doing? They say "FINE!" while rolling their eyes and making a huge sigh. Even though they might have stated that they are doing "fine", through their non-verbal communication you know that this is not the case. **Often what is coming out of our mouths is either ignored or overshadowed because of our non-verbal communication.**

For your exercise, identify the Angry Non-Verbal Communication tactic that you currently use by circling it. Next, circle the Productive Non-Verbal Communication tactics you will begin practicing.

Angry Non-Verbal Communication	Productive Non-Verbal Communication
Rolling eyes or glaring	Direct yet appropriate eye contact
Smirking, Scowling, Grimacing	Smiling or neutral facial expression
Pounding on a table, kicking objects, throwing things, folding arms, hands on hips	Nodding or physically turning toward the speaker
Yelling or screaming	Speaking in a calm, audible tone of voice
Pushing, shoving, hitting, blocking the path of the speaker	Keeping an appropriate distance from the speaker

18

Just Breathe!

TEMPER TAMING TIPS
The College Student's Guide to
Anger Intelligence™

Just Breathe!

The movie "Bad Boys II" popularized the pseudo-anger management technique called "woosa". One of the main characters in the movie played by Martin Lawrence used the "technique" in an effort to calm down and manage his anger.

In addition to that, I know you have heard, seen or tried the popular anger management technique of taking deep breaths. Usually, when someone has said something that triggers your temper – you may be either count to 10 or take shallow (or deep) breaths for a few seconds and still proceed with your tirade! Contrary to popular opinion and movies and television, this technique doesn't work usually because you are not breathing in the right manner to actually calm yourself down. Shallow breathing can lead to even more irritability. **Deep breathing has been known to reduce stress, increase focus and promote a good night's rest.** It can also help you study better, stay focused on assignments and feel less tired. It is important to learn some deep breathing exercises and to practice them at least once per day.

Deep-Breathing Exercises

This exercise can help keep your anger from getting out of control. Practice these at least once a day.

Steps

1. Sit comfortably or lie on your back.

2. Breathe in slowly and deeply for a count of 7.

3. Hold your breath for count of 7.

4. Breathe out slowly for a count of 7, pushing out all the air.

5. Repeat several times until you feel calm and relaxed.

19

Stress Less

TEMPER TAMING TIPS
The College Student's Guide to
Anger Intelligence™

Stress Less

R ight now as a college student you might be feeling stressed out by school work, relationships and new financial responsibilities. When you are experiencing high levels of stress – it can intensify your anger. For instance, let's say you have a mid-term exam coming up and you really need to get a "B" on it to keep your scholarship. If you lose this scholarship, you will likely have to leave college. While attempting to study, your roommate is in the other room laughing and talking with a group of friends. You ask them to quiet down a couple of times but the last time you start screaming and threatening them and it almost leads to a physical altercation. The real issue here is not so much the roommate but the fact that there was stress about staying in school underlying the situation.

One excellent way to handle stress is to acknowledge the stressors in your life. Sometimes we are really not aware of the issues that are bothering us. Below is a list of common stressors including School, Relationships, Family, Finances, etc. Check off those that you are currently experiencing.

__ Academics
__ Financial Issues
__ Work Concerns (includes conflict & unemployment issues)
__ Family Problems (issues with children, siblings, parents, etc.)
__ Relationship Problems (issues with girlfriend or boyfriend)
__ Health Concerns (illnesses, etc.)
__ Other_____

20 Ways to Control Stress – Pick one that you can use this week

Do only one thing at a time instead of multi-tasking.	Slow down. Talk slowly.
Focus only on the present and what you can do now.	Establish & maintain a daily schedule that is realistic.
Exercise!	Get adequate sleep, rest and nutrition.
Say "No" more often.	Don't try to know all the answers.
Talk less, listen more.	Learn to meet your own needs.
Always have a plan B.	SMILE!
Ask questions.	Simplify, simplify, simplify.
Do nothing that leads you to tell a lie.	Be prepared to wait.
Ask for help if you feel over-whelmed.	Do unpleasant tasks early in the day.
Eliminate destructive self-talk.	Allow quiet time for yourself.

20

Stop Being a Control Freak

TEMPER TAMING TIPS
The College Student's Guide to
Anger Intelligence™

Stop Being a Control Freak!

When you are upset with your boyfriend or girlfriend do you yell at them, call them names, or even push or hit them? If so, you are engaging in abusive behaviors. Emotional Abuse is when you try to control someone by saying nasty or mean things to them. So much of what we say to those we say we love the most is actually considered emotional abuse. On the other hand, physical abuse occurs when you try to control your each other by hitting, pushing, destroying things, etc. Both are equally harmful!

Dating abuse and anger are NOT the same. When you use your anger to gain control of your significant other you are being abusive. Instead of trying to control others, control yourself or you might find yourself in some serious circumstances that will not only jeopardize your education, your future career and your relationships but also your freedom.

Do you use any of these tactics in your relationship to control your partner?

Name Calling
Put-downs
Insults
Yelling/Screaming
Threats of violence
Racial slurs
Stalking
Blackmail
Embarrassing someone
Spreading rumors
Controlling someone
Unwanted sexual comments
Preventing social interactions
Threatening to commit suicide

IF YOU ARE USING ANY OF THESE TACTICS, GET HELP BY CONTACTING YOUR CAMPUS COUNSELING CENTER!

IF THESE TACTICS ARE HAPPENING TO YOU CONTACT YOUR CAMPUS COUNSELING CENTER OR CALL THE DOMESTIC VIOLENCE HOTLINE AT 1-800-799-SAFE!

21

THINK B4 U TXT

TEMPER TAMING TIPS
The College Student's Guide to
Anger Intelligence™

THINK B4 U TXT

Texting is the most popular form of communication for most college and high school students. It is a great way to stay in touch with family and friends! But it can also be excessive, for example just a few years ago there was a 16 year old girl who sent over 6,000 text messages in one month!

Texting has also become one of the most misunderstood forms of communication as well. If you have ever sent a text message that someone took the wrong way, then you know what I mean. Often we fire off messages in anger later having to explain our outburst or apologizing for it. Frequently in anger we use text messages and other forms of digital communication to vent our frustrations, which is not always a good idea. **When you receive an inflammatory text message – instead of responding right away use a Timeout Text Tactic.**

Time Out Text Tactics

Choose one of the tactics below when responding to a text message that has made you angry

*Write the text then delete it.

*Take 10 minutes before your respond.

*Text the person back and tell them you that you will respond to them later. (#notrightnow)

*Ignore it.

22

Don't Be Bitter

TEMPER TAMING TIPS
The College Student's Guide to
Anger Intelligence™

Don't Be Bitter

B itterness… What do you think when you hear that term? Personally, I think of it as a weed in a lovely garden. Growing up, my grandmother had a rock garden, which obviously didn't require much care but served its purpose of beautifying her yard. She hated when weeds would spring up in her landscape. She even took care to lay plastic underneath the rocks to stop the growth, however, the weeds somehow and at some point inevitably popped up through the plastic and ruined my grandmother's rock masterpiece!

It may seem like a trivial story; however, that's how bitterness crops up. It doesn't come around, at least initially, where it can be seen. It's not one of the most obvious emotions. **But once it rears its ugly head, it can cause more destruction to the person harboring the bitterness than to those around them.**

So how do you know if you are bitter? Here are five ways to know if you are allowing the weeds of bitterness to spring up in your life:

When you hear a certain person's name, your whole mood changes.

The mention or thought of a particular situation or person puts an ugly expression on your face.

People tell you often, "You need to get over it!"

When you begin talking about a certain situation, it turns into a long, drawn out rant and others begin yawning, rolling their eyes, changing the subject, or suddenly have to leave your presence.

When you encounter the object of your bitterness, your body begins to react. Your heart beats fast, your palms get sweaty or your face may turn red among other reactions.

If see yourself in any of these statements, you might be bitter. Go back and search through the other tactics in this book to rid yourself of bitterness.

23

Let it GO!

TEMPER TAMING TIPS
The College Student's Guide to
Anger Intelligence™

Let it GO!

I n 2008, a mother and her two sons were brutally murdered and the only surviving members of the family left were the father and a 16 year old daughter. When the dust settled, the 16 year old daughter was the mastermind of the event which as actually committed by her boyfriend and his friend. They were upset because her parents made them break up since they believed he was a bad influence on her.

When it came time for sentencing, the death penalty was put on the table. Instead of the father supporting that sentence, he forgave them because he realized that giving them the death penalty would not bring his family back. If he could forgive such a horrific act, how much more could you forgive those who have hurt you?

Forgiveness is not about forgetting or pretending something didn't happen. It is about releasing the other party from the debt that you feel they owe you. The more you feel like someone owes (an apology, money, attention, time, etc) you, the least likely you are to forgive them. The more we hold on to it the more we hold on to negative energy. Negative effects of holding on to unforgiveness are distraction, fatigue, introvertedness and the list goes on. Let it go and move on with your life…I'm sure they have moved on with theirs.

"Holding on to past hurts only hurts you!"

Write a list of people you need to forgive for you to let go and move on with your life.

24

Mind Your Mood

TEMPER TAMING TIPS
The College Student's Guide to
Anger Intelligence™

Mind Your Mood

H as this ever happened to you? *You wake up in a great mood! You've had a good weekend: you relaxed with friends, had your favorite meal at one of your favorite restaurants and you've decided that this week is going to be an awesome week! The first person you encounter is your RA, who has a huge smile on her face and exchanges chitchat with you. You make a few more "Good Mornings", with a little pep in your step. Then you see one of your study partners who already has a grimace on his face. You say "Good Morning" and he says, "I guess..." and then launches into how horrible his weekend was and why he didn't even want to come study this morning. In just two minutes, you begin to feel your great mood dwindling- it's been contaminated by your study partner's negative mood. Your great weekend feeling has melted away and now you just want to get the day over with rather than get it started.*

That was a long way of describing how our moods can not only change quickly but how moods are contagious. Often our negative moods with others can be those that spread like wildfire. That's why it is important to be mindful of them.

1 Hour Mood Minding Experiment

So now that you have a little more information about why it is important to mind your mood, here is a little experiment for you to see how aware you are of your mood and its effects on others.

1. For the next hour check in with yourself to see what kind of mood you are in. At the end of the hour, check to see if your mood has changed and why or why not.

2. Think about one person within the one hour time frame whose mood YOU might be influencing. How would you change your mood to make sure it has a positive effect?

3. Be attentive to the body language and facial expressions that you are displaying to others during this time.

What did you notice? Did you see how your mood affected someone else's? Did your mood change because someone else was in a different mood? Continue to monitor this on a regular basis.

25

Adjust Your Expectations

TEMPER TAMING TIPS
The College Student's Guide to
Anger Intelligence™

Adjust Your Expectations

One of the biggest causes of conflict and anger are unmet and unrealistic expectations. Don't get me wrong, I'm not saying not to have expectations, but quite often they are not always rational. We become disappointed by what we think people **should** do, how they **should** treat us and how they **should** act, instead of being realistic and realizing that we have no power or control over any of these things.

I know a college junior who always complains about the lateness of her financial aid net check. Each semester, she receives the same amount (that's usually the wrong amount) and she has to visit the students account office to correct it. Yet each and every time she goes, she becomes verbally aggressive with the staff. One semester, she became so enraged at a staff person that she received a police escort off campus. She could have avoided that embarrassing episode if she would have been realistic about her previous experience with the student accounts office.

If the same things continuously anger you, then it might be a good idea to change your expectations of it to reduce your level of anger and to decrease your stress.

Here are 7 tips that might assist you in becoming more realistic with your expectations:

1. Realize that people are human and imperfect and they WILL make mistakes AND so will you.

2. Not every situation will turn out the way you want it and if it doesn't it is NOT the end of the world.

3. Compromise, negotiate, and collaborate as often as you can because at the end of the day, we won't always get what we want all of the time.

4. Be Easy! Don't be so hard on yourself. I myself am a victim of "I should have done better". You may have done the best you could at the time and know that the next time you will do better.

5. Don't put anyone or anything on a pedestal, if you do, you are sure to be disappointed.

6. Talk to whomever disappointed you; let them know how you feel in an assertive manner.

7. Set realistic boundaries. Let others know what is accepted within these limits and what is not. But even if they go out of bounds, it is not the end of the world. You might learn something about yourself in the process.

Accepting people and situations as they are is hard, no doubt. However, if you are often frustrated due to your expectations not being met, then doing the hard work of changing the way you think may not be a bad idea.

26

Know WHO to be Mad At!

TEMPER TAMING TIPS
The College Student's Guide to
Anger Intelligence™

Know WHO to be Mad At!

Often times we become angry or upset with our significant other or loved ones when we are really upset about something else. Or we chew the head off of our roommate but we are really not happy about what's going on in our relationship. Or give the cashier a hard time about the length of the line, or being too slow, or not having the peanut butter we came in for, when we're really mad at ourselves.

All of these are classic examples of displaced anger. I know this may not be proper grammar, but the idea here is to "know WHO to be mad at!" Or to put it more succinctly, target your anger to its rightful owner. You won't solve the problem by being upset with the wrong people. It ruins relationships, friendships, reputations and could even cost you the career plan to obtain once you graduate.

There are many reasons why we don't express our anger to the right individuals. We may be intimidated by the other person, feel powerless, or may be unsure and/or unable to express ourselves and our anger effectively. The next activity will give you some pointers on how to make sure we don't displace our anger onto the wrong target.

Here are a few ways that you can use your anger intelligence to avoid displacing your anger onto the wrong person.

Uncover the "Real" issue - What are you REALLY upset about? Anger is a secondary emotion and there is another feeling beneath (hurt, disappointment, fear, confusion, etc.) it that is driving the frustrations.

Practice Assertive Communication - When you're upset with someone and you have the right tools, you can let them know how you feel in an appropriate manner. (See tip #9 *"Be Assertive".*)

Take a Time Out - If you know that you are stressed or upset about something, take some time to cool off or think about the issue before you engage. (See tip #11 *"Take a Time Out".*)

www.ingramcontent.com/pod-product-compliance
Lightning Source LLC
Chambersburg PA
CBHW060122050426
42448CB00010B/1999